Norbert Hirschhorn

To Sing Away the Darkest Days

Poems Re-imagined from Yiddish Folksongs

[handwritten: בתצו / Goldberg]

[handwritten: For a wonderful day in the park.]

[handwritten signature] 11 Sept 2016

Holland Park Press

Published by Holland Park Press 2013

First Edition

A CIP catalogue record for this book is
available from The British Library.

ISBN 978-1-907320-35-4

Cover designed by Reactive Graphics

Printed and bound in Great Britain by
CPI Antony Rowe, Chippenham and Eastbourne

www.hollandparkpress.co.uk

To Sing Away the Darkest Days is the culmination of a five-year project which saw Norbert Hirschhorn source more than one thousand Yiddish songs from several archives and from collections on the Internet, as well as from CD's.

Ruth Rubin, pioneer archivist of Yiddish folksong, wrote: 'Yiddish folksongs are in a vernacular closest to the popular speech of the folk'.

For Norbert, they helped him to rediscover and trace his own Jewish cultural history. However, some of the songs 'spoke' to him as a poet and begged for a new translation, or 're-imagining' as he calls it, into English poems.

The resulting collection tells the story of the emigrant, the Jew in the Diaspora, while drawing on the poet's own experience. The poems are both poignant and humorous, capturing the Jewish experience; but the struggle and questioning of the poet add an extra intensity.

To Sing Away the Darkest Days is not only a wonderful collection of poems but also a necessary historical document.

For my brother Larry and sister Linda; and in memory of our parents

CONTENTS

9

INTRODUCTION

Yiddish was the principal daily language of European Jews for nearly one thousand years. Yiddish is an expression of the dispersal of the people through many lands: a fusion language based on Middle High German and written in Hebrew script, with additional vocabulary and syntax from Slavic, Hebrew, Aramaic, and other sources. From the sixteenth century, and especially during the nineteenth and early twentieth centuries, a rich literature developed, comprising song, fiction, poetry, disputation and polemic, as well as politics, and national and social movements. The language was nearly extinguished by the Shoah, remaining today as the daily vernacular of only a remnant of the Jewish people – chiefly Hasidim and elderly survivors of the Holocaust. The past four decades, however, have seen a revival of Yiddish as a cultural phenomenon: language courses are now given at major universities, and Yiddish phrases, humour and music are common parlance among Jews and many non-Jews – perhaps also as a reassertion of Diaspora Jewry against the hegemonic rule of Hebrew in the State of Israel.

Folksongs in Yiddish existed as far back as the fourteenth century. But the genre flourished from the eighteenth century onward, first with the rise of ecstatic Hasidic prayer, and then generally in the Russian Empire's Pale of Settlement, which included the old Lithuanian and Polish empires, to which Jews were banished until the 1917 revolution. Conditions there were appalling: persecution, pogroms, military conscription, and poverty. The thousands of Yiddish folksongs reflected the condition of the people: their hopes, prayer and daily lives, and provided biting social commentary. 'Yiddish folksongs are in a vernacular closest to the popular speech of the folk', wrote Ruth Rubin, pioneer archivist of Yiddish folksong. '[I]nto folksong were poured feelings, thoughts, desires, aspirations, which often seemingly had no other place to go'.[1] In the most desperate time, the people were 'singing for survival'. Now, as Gila Flam notes, Yiddish folksongs also serve as commemoration of that horrid time.[2]

Some folksongs began as poems; some became poems adapted from the songs. (In Yiddish *lid* means both song and poem.) The folksongs were, in any event, fluid, shape shifting, often altered and adapted in passage from one person, time, or circumstance to another.

As a Jew rediscovering his own cultural history, and as a poet, I noticed that English translations of the folksongs' lyrics, unlike translations of Yiddish poetry, are mainly dutiful, stilted, capturing little of the rich idiom and feeling of the original; certainly none of the felicitous rhyming or cadence as conveyed in both the language and the melody.

[1] *Yiddish Folksongs from the Ruth Rubin Archive*, edited by Chana Mlotek and Mark Slobin (Detroit: Wayne State University Press, 2007; pp. 16, xii).

[2] Gila Flam, *Singing for Survival: Songs of the Lodz Ghetto, 1940–1945*. (Champaign, IL: University of Illinois Press, 1991). [My grandmothers died in the Lodz Ghetto.]

For this project I had to train myself to read Yiddish more or less fluently, with a Yiddish–English dictionary by my side, and to listen to dozens of Yiddish folksongs on CD's and the Internet. What made it easier was my working knowledge of German, but more importantly it was my heritage in a home where, despite little Yiddish actually being spoken, my parents' attitudes, intonations, superstitions and – above all – memories surrounded me. It is no coincidence that Yiddish is known as the *mame-loshen*, the mother tongue.

Thus, as I scoured more than one thousand song texts from several archives, and from collections on the Internet and CD's, many 'spoke' to me, like a daimon, begging for 're-imagination', as I term it. Entering into the lyrics to distil their essence – to advance, enlarge, and, sometimes, subvert the original in order to create a vibrant poem in English.

BASHERTE*
(*Two roads diverged in a yellow wood...*
and I – I took the one less traveled by,
And that has made all the difference – Robert Frost)

And I, I escaped from Vienna to London – the War –
then Manhattan where I grew up, became a doctor,
marrying M, a Catholic, which made my parents cry.
Yearning to cure the world, I flew to Egypt, divorced, met C –
an anthropologist – fell in love: this the one true road I've
traveled.

And I escaped from Vienna to Palestine where I grew up,
became a GP. Yearning to heal the world I practiced
in the Negev, met C – an anthropologist studying Bedouin
traditions – fell in love, joining the road I've traveled.

Escaped from Vienna, but not New York or Palestine,
grew up in London, a GP, married my classmate's
sister E. Our careers estranged us. Yearning
to restore my world I turned to public health, met C –
an anthropologist teaching Bedouin culture – fell in love,
crossing against the light.

15

Instead of M, Catholic, I married a cousin's friend N,
whose warm Jewish family nestled me into suburban medicine:
big house, big pool, Cadillac DeVille; made my parents proud.
When N grew morose, I starved. Yearning to escape my world,
I just walked away, turning to public health, where I met
C, my Pole Star, on the only road I've traveled by.

* The destined one.

CAVE SONG

Tell me, Maran, my brother,
where will you hold your seder?
In a grotto, on a high bluff,
there will I prepare my seder.

But Maran, how will you
ever find unleavened bread?
In that cavern, by God's own hand,
matzos are already baking.

Say, Maran, who will provide
our holy Haggadah?
In the catacomb, a cranny –
there have I long kept one hidden.

Yet Maran, who will save you
when our foes hear your singing?
When Inquisitors come to seize me,
I will drown them in my song.

An Ashkenazi Jew encounters a Sephardi *Converso*, a Jew forced by the
Spanish Inquisition to become Christian, but who resists by keeping Jewish
rituals in secret; here, the Passover celebration. *Maran* is the Yiddish word
for 'Marrano', meaning 'pig' whose unclean flesh Conversos now had to eat.

TEN BROTHERS

Ten brothers jobbing kosher wine, one kicked the bucket,
    then there were nine.
Nine brothers hauling iron freight, one of us run over,
    that made eight.
Eight brothers running a tavern, one dead drunk,
    and so there were seven.
Seven brothers into politics, one shot dead,
    bang! suddenly but six.

Lenin mitn fiddle, Trotsky mitn bass,
    sing a little ditty for the working class.

Six brothers, Yiddish-y jive, one shoved off to Belsen,
    the remnant was five.
Five brothers peddling shmattas door to door, one got mugged,
    leaving only four.
Four brothers stepped out to pee, one struck by lightning,
    now we were three.
Three brothers, déjà vu, one bought the farm,
    down to just two.

Lenin mitn fiddle, Trotsky mitn bass,
    sing a little ditty for the working class.

Two brothers – engraving names in headstones –
and when you died, there was me, alone.

Lenin mitn fiddle, Trotsky mitn bass,
sing a little ditty for the working class.

MAKE A LIVING

(All Jewish folksongs are about Jewish tailors – Zero
Mostel)

I'm a little tailor –
   good, cheerful, brave,
      stitching something from nothing,
two groschen and a kopek,
   enough for bread
     without any butter.

I'm a little cobbler –
   not so good, brain is boiling,
      nails in my mouth,
leather tough, life tougher,
   never mind the kids,
     I go barefoot.

I'm a little pushcart puller
   shouting *buy! onions! buy!*
      no, lady, no raisins, no almonds,
two groschen and she wants...
   so I wrap my tallith about me, bless God,
     and cry out: *buy! onions! buy!*

   aydl-bydl-didi-didi-dam
     oy-doy-doy-diri-diri-tam
   ay-bay-bay-bidi-bidi-bam

THREE SISTERS

work the streets of Leicester Square
shilling to all who pass through, though
seeing none. One peddles ribbons
'for your sweetie's hair', the next
hawks roses filched from front gardens,
and the eldest sells something at once
too cheap, too dear.

The younger ones won't hate this sister –
First feed the face. Then talk right and wrong.
Back at the bedsit they wet their merchandise
with tears.

The Little Stove

A hut on chicken legs, a little stove, a rebbe
    teaching three-year olds their
        ABCs, the *Aleph-Beys*. Teaching,
            teaching three-year olds! Pay attention

little ones, think on it, my lambs, what
    it is you're learning here. Say it,
        say it again. Children, you musn't
            be afraid, every Torah lesson will be

hard paid. *Nu*, what else do our people
    need? Say it, say it again. As you drag
        the weight of exile, you,
            my treasures, will be

dispirited, you'll be plagued, but
    courage comes through *Aleph-Beys,* so
        say those letters, say them again. When you
            grow up, my dears, you'll learn how these

letters fetch sorrow, fetch tears.

I
lady wid a baby
named him liddle Abie
fed him bread and gravy
drove the neighbors crazy

rocked him in a shoebox
'til he died of chickenpox

II
Hey hey mamma
Cat's into the butter
Hens ain't laying eggs
Bride's got hairy legs
Rich man wears a shawl
Beggar's got none at all
Children gnaw their fingers
Mothers die of hunger

From My Mouth

A destitute widow, daughter of Zion, huddled
in a corner room in the synagogue where

men study and pray, murmurs
a lullaby to her only child.

A little goat
settles under her feet, returned

from foraging scraps in the market.
G-d forbid, the widow whispers,

this be your calling – hauling
a pushcart, crying out your wares:

Onions! Buy onions! Let it instead happen –
from my mouth to His ear – you will be rich,

or a scholar, but that you will never forget.
Now sleep little one, sleep.

FROM PODWOLOCZYSKA TO ELLIS ISLAND

Say, sweet one,
how will you manage
on this long, penniless journey?

> *I'll run every street*
> *shouting, 'I do washing! Washing!'*
> *as long as I journey with you.*

Say, pretty one,
where will you find wash water
on this long, grubby journey?

> *I'll wash in streams,*
> *rivers, the sea,*
> *as long as I journey with you.*

But my treasure,
you'll need to eat
on this long, hungry journey.

> *Bread and salt,*
> *two will eat as one,*
> *as long as I journey with you.*

You sleep on feathers –
where will you lay your head
on this long, tiring journey?

On straw, wood, earth.
I'm young, I'm strong.
I intend to journey with you.

Earth? Wood? Straw?
Then what for covers
on this long, cold journey?

Moon, stars, open sky
and your warm self will do,
for as long as I journey with you.

MY COUSIN THE GREENHORN

I had a pretty cousin, just over on the boat, a real greenhorn. Her hair cascaded in curls, her cheeks flushed with freedom, she was the kind who skipped when she walked, trilled when she talked. 'Listen greenhorn', I warned, 'this may be the *goldene medine*, but it's no land of milk and honey. The streets are pocked, the men are goats, you've no *mama* no *tate* to watch out for you.' Yet her feet begged to dance, her eyes to flirt, and no bent-backed tailor or pale Talmudic scholar for her, God forbid! But you can't eat gaiety. Soon she was tied to a machine, working for some lecher himself once green. Meantime, I had my own troubles, so when I saw her again her feet were wrapped in ragged slippers, her hair cut blunt, her cheeks, once like pomegranates, now sunken and sallow, her belly swollen. 'Nu, greenhorn, how goes it?' She stared past me as if not knowing that anyone spoke. Finally: 'To hell with your *goldene medine*'.

goldene medine – land of gold

Mayn Rue-Plats (My Resting Place)

Don't seek for me
   where myrtles green
      not there my darling
         but bent to my machine.

Don't come searching
   when the cuckoo calls
      I've not long within
         these sweatshop's walls.

Please don't find me
   in a fountain's spray
      they are just my tears
         veiling all days grey.

But if you love me
   you'll set a stone
      here where I rest
         my silent home.

ABECEDARIAN FOR THE WORKERS OF THE WORLD

Rich men dine on artichokes
Poor men choke on beans

Rich men quaff champagne
Poor men swallow dregs

Rich men rub elbows
Poor men soak their feet

Rich men throw garden galas
Poor men shelter in hovels

Rich men collect ivory
Poor men jailed for stealing junk

Rich men's wealth swung by karma
Poor men's bread wrung from labour

Rich men's lives a melody
Poor men's lives a joyless noise

Rich men's wives show off opals
Poor men's wives make do with paste

Rich men sleep at ease under quilts
Poor men lie rigid under rags

Rich men work the poor like slaves
Poor men prepare their Thermopylae

Rich men exploit unrelentingly
Poor men their short-lived victims

Rich men take the waters in winter
Poor men queue for soup at Xmas

Rich men own yachts
Poor men own zilch

i.m. John Rety

Hey pussy cat, why such a pout?
You just checked up your pedigree?
So, what did you find out? Your daddy
greases palms at City Hall. Your momma's
a shoplifter. Little brother fixes ball games,
and sister's run off with a grifter.
                    Uh huh.
Your uncle takes bets in his pajamas,
auntie peddles shmatta snitched from tailors.
Big brother's cooling in the slammer
and big sister services sailors.
                    There's more?
Your *zayde* butchers pork for kosher, and *bobe*
runs a whorehouse and you could be anyone's
mamzer, a foundling snatched from a doss-house.
What a wanky life.

zayde – grandfather; *bobe* – grandmother; *mamzer* – bastard

A Czarist Conscript Bids Farewell

Be well, dear parents, I'm off
To a faraway place – treeless,
Windburnt, where no bird sings,
No rooster salutes the morning.

Cry not, dear parents,
But forgive your son
If he does not keep kosher –
Pig and potatoes is all they serve.

Stay whole, dear parents,
Even as I leave you. May
God grant you well-being

All the years of your lives.

Call me Yosl Ber. You can call me *pisher,* it's sweet fuck-all to
me. I used to be a cobbler's lackey licking boot soles, dawn to
dark. Now I've joined the Czarist army and clomp around in
combats. I eat regular in the army, pork sausage with cheese.
In the shtetl when a Jew eats a chicken, one of them is sick.

What do Jews ever inherit but hemorrhoids and heartburn? I
wear a uniform, I carry a gun. When a worm sits in
horseradish it thinks it's in heaven. Nine rabbis can't make a
minyan, but they'll take ten of the likes of me. They hate me,
those whiskers, declare me a *meshumad,* spouting Talmud
from their mouths like turds from a goat. They should run to
the toilet every three minutes. They should grow like onions
with their heads in the dirt.

To be a Jew is like being buried in the ground baking bagels.
But being in the Czarist army, ah! a resurrection. I can go to
any tavern in my fine uniform, boots and sword and give the
barmaid a wink. And she'll give me a wink. And then we'll
wink together. For a glass of milk, you don't have to buy the
whole cow.

minyan – gathering of ten men required to begin prayers
meshumad – apostate

SCAPEGOATS

Two little beasts, trussed upon
a cart, on their way to slaughter,

seized by the High Priest,
penance for sins of the People.

hey, dona dona ha ha ha

One a burnt offering to Yahweh,
the other thrown from a cliff –

limbs shattered, organs ruptured –
sacrifices to purify the Tribe.

hey, dona dona ha ha ha

Hey! No such elegy. Cancel
the calamity, obliterate the catastrophe –

let the goats gnaw through the bonds,
cast down the drover, bind up the butcher,

let ravens hoik out their eyes.
Then shall all cry out to angels:
The Jewish People live.

hey, dona dona ha ha ha

A Yiddishe Mama Laments

So now he sends me this song, *A Yidishe Mama.* Me, who
fed him from my breast, rocked him in his cradle, wiped his
tuchas, kissed his bruises, held his head when he threw up,
made his bed, brushed his hair, cleaned his face with my
spit, stitched holes in his socks, fed him meatloaf I didn't eat
myself, watched from the window for his coming home it
shouldn't be too late, made him do his homework – so proud
if he got an 'A' why not, my prince, my darling, my scholar.
Then he runs off with a *shiksa* – and sends me this song. By
me, he's dead already.

A MARXIST LULLABY

Asleep, at last, my child?
Now I can sing my lullaby:
    Someday you will know
What means poor, what means rich.

lyu lyu lyu lyu lyu

    Palaces! Mansions!
Who builds them?
    We do.
Who lives in them?
    They do.

lyu lyu lyu lyu lyu

Cellars for likes of us –
    Bedbugs, roaches, mould –
Why you caught polio,
    A never-ending cold.

Asleep at last, my child, asleep?

lyu lyu lyu lyu lyu

SLEEP MY CHILD

My life, my only Kaddish,
   your father's in America where
      people eat challah even weekdays.

     ay lyu-u-lyu-u-li

               Ludlow Street, tenement,
                  filthy room, that's where
                     your father lives.

He'll send us twenty dollars,
   he'll send his picture too. Someday,
      he'll send for us, America.

    lyu-u-lyu-u-li

               Starved, weak, soup kitchens:
                  stale bread, no meat,
                     he feeds on smoke.

I'll make for you some
   chicken soup while we wait
      for the happy letter.

    lyu-u-lyu-u-li

Layoffs, a bitter time. He has to
come home, has to
borrow for the boat.

Your mother sits by your cradle
and cries. One day, you'll know
what she really meant.

ay lyu-u-lyu-li

A Yiddish Divorce

The bitterest wind torments a street.

Good evening sister –
I bring you bad news.
Your husband in America
says for you, he no longer has use.

The lacerating wind penetrates a house.

He no longer wants to know you.
Here is paper, from his own pen:
Your husband in America
says *You are permitted to all men.*

An icicle wind impales a heart.

Three children do cartwheels
out in the yard.

THE LAST BRANCH PLEADS FOR RELEASE

All I want is to return to soil.
Let birds repair to some other nests.
Let the wind carry me to my final hour.
My Lord has surrendered our roots,
Gone to ruin, yet demands I carry on.
He must think we're a banyan or baobab!

Let me be, beguiling dream,
You'll soon have me hearing again those
Beloved calls – trills, warbles,
Carols, cackles – and me greening
The world. Ah, too late. I am a quivering
Last branch of a last old tree in a last old forest.

My haunted verse will be heard as crackles
In a woodsman's pyre.

i.m. Rhona Rapoport

THE NEIGHBOURING VILLAGE

We hear their songs no more, sung
by a people put to flight, hymns

from a village destroyed by war.

We used to visit door to door under olive
trees, forbidden now to shelter their families.

A fuss of roosters shrieked all night.

We hear their songs no more, perhaps
just a village done in by war. Did it

matter so they weren't us? Who forced us,

who stopped our ears against the cries
from a village wiped off the maps,

its town clock rent silent.

ECCLESIASTES REDUX

vapour of vapours
    shadow and cloud
inanity of inanities
    mosquito in your ear
fly up your nose

vapour of vapours
    Cain was unable
his bonfire smoke heavier than
    air unfair
miasma not plasma except in
    astrophysics
nebulous nebulae
    incubus succubus
as long as you love your mother

vapour of vapours
    effluvius, Jupiter Pluvius
insanity of insanities
    steam in your dream
urbanity manatee profanity and
    not to forget Christianity

vapour of vapours
   village idiots
I'm the square root of two
   irrational number
golden-haired ratio
a Miss American pi computed
   to ten trillion digits
what does WW eleven stand for?

The Hebrew word *hevl,* translated in the King James Version as 'vanity',
has its root in the word for breath; and cognate with the name Abel.

For Sure

Lookit, Mama, Papa's bought me this velour.
I'll have a Russian manteau made, haute couture.

What? Is he crazy? We're supposed to be poor.
Mama, he intends for me a proper catch, not some boor.

Oy veh, next you'll be getting a pedicure...
Why not, Mama, I mean to be pretty, I plan to allure.

Prancing about town with some paramour...
No, Mama, my eye's on the banker's son, Issur.

I only know what men want, to get into your...
Oh, Mama, honestly, I promise to keep pure.

Nu, so what's to come from this shmatta velour?
I'll be Mrs. Banker, the Grand Tour, Baden-Baden,

the water cure, for sure.

Bundle on a stick, satchel
on my back. What

else do I need? What else? A hut with
seven small fry, a goat, and eleven

kopeks, what else do I need? The rain
slaps against the window, squalor

whistles down the chimney.
What? What else do I need? Lost

my moxie, down on luck, I jump from
rebbe to rebbe, not one helps.

Who needs? Who needs you?

The Quantum Rebbe

Nu, Einstein, with your ferret's brain,
come sit at our Rebbe's table and learn
a thing or two. So you made a rocket

to shoot at the stars? Which makes you
a wonder? Ha! Our Rebbe opens his
umbrella and he's dancing on Mars.

You discovered relativity? Our Rebbe can fly
faster than light to greet the *shabbos* bride
from the previous night, returns looking younger.

Don't beat the kettle about your Big Bang!
Who do you think was virtually there when G-d,
Master of the Universe, created time, heaven, earth!

And when the *moshiyekh,* the Anointed One,
comes to rebuild our Temple, our Rebbe will be
alongside – sanctifying, cantillating, praying.

When Our Rebbe...

Sha, still, make no commotion,
when our Rebbe starts to dance,
like piety in motion – our Rebbe

rhapsodic, enchanted... Sha,
don't make a racket – we clap
when our Rebbe whirls, tap

our feet, ecstatic... Sha,
still, the Rebbe's about to sing. When
he chants the holy songs, our whole

earth rings and the Devil will die.
Sha, be still.

TRISTESSE

The golden peacock flew to us, flew
while night opened its golden eye.
Sleep my radiant love.

Night opened its golden eye, while I,
violin, played melodies with your bow.
Sleep my sweet-natured love.

I, violin, played melodies with your bow
when Fortune, bewitched, shone her face on us.
Sleep my unquiet love.

Fortune, fickle, abandons us,
the golden peacock has flown.
O sad love, our night is gone.

*In Yiddish legend, the golden peacock is a messenger carrying greetings to
loved ones.*

To Life!

A little nip, l'khayim! and why not,
    drink to friends and friendship,
        and for l'khayim, hooray!

Three little nips:
    for oldsters shmoozing,
        youngsters dancing hora,
            shnorrers with their chutzpah.

A little nip, l'khayim! – we shouldn't lose the glow
    to sing away the darkest days
        that always come, seldom go. Another

nip, l'khayim! to every
    mother, including mine, *nakhes*
        from their little nippers. Now

just a wee nip to keep that
    fragrance, l'khayim, on your lips; one
        last nip, l'khayim, for what
            we always dream of.

nakhes – pleasure, joy; *shnorrer* – a panhandler

CONFESSIONS

In the old country my grandfather stayed
up that silent, holy night, dealing '21'

to ward off the flying messiah, rudely
known as *Yoshke Pandre*. Hanukah could never

match an incandescent supernova drawing
magi in caravans to the pale virgin,

that halo glowing on the babe, sheep
on their knees. No side-locked rebbe

widdershins down the chimney
with presents for good little *boytshiks*

and *meydlekh* – unless he's
come to check your kitchen for *kashruth*.

Union Square, Hanukah: Lubavitchers light
up a giant *menorah*. Even with his

back turned, he knew, and whirled
about – *Are you Jewish?* he asked. If

I'd said yes, he'd haul me
into the Mitsvahmobile, make me

lay *tefillin*, promise to divorce my *shiksa* wife,
eat kosher for the rest of my life. Meanwhile,

kitty-corner across the Square, in the crèche,
the Holy Family lovingly refused

to reconvert. No, I said for the first
time in my life. He asked me again,

Are you Jewish?
No, no, no.

II
In Jerusalem pale scholars mine biblical
blueprints to rebuild the Temple.

First: blow up the Dome of the Rock.
Then: the *Al Aqsa* mosque. A pious

man in broad-brimmed *shtreiml*,
caftan and *payess* holds up a cell-phone

to the Western Wall so his cousin in Golders Green
can call in a prayer to God. *Do you*

still believe in prayer, my Likudnik
cousin asks. *I count on my gun*

more than God, he says,
staring off to the low-scalloped hills.

He has a point: How could
someone kill six million of us

by gas, guns, clubs, ice, lice, pus,
and breaking stone... just so someone could say

'it never happened'. I hate
what my cousin says, who believes

we are God's Chosen People.
I wonder what we were chosen for.

The privilege.

III
Diaspora, dispersion, from the Greek,
to scatter, to sow. We flourish like wildflowers,

weeds, accidentals, everywhere broadcast.
Chinese food in Chinatown, pizza Little Italy,

kasha knishes at Yonah Schimmel's on Houston Street.
The Diaspora is good: keep, nourish, savour, spread it.

Thank God for the Romans. Without Diaspora
Jews would be some curious episode,

taught in Ancient Civilizations 101.
An old theater trick – say

the word *Jew,* and a shudder
ripples the audience.

IV
Blacks wanting education,
American Indians refusing the rez,
dissed as oreos, apples: white within.

Jews criticizing Israel,

excoriated as *self-hating:*
oy on their lips, *goy* in their guts.

V
Thus saith the LORD of hosts. Now go and smite Amalek, and
utterly destroy all that they have, and spare them not; but
slay both man and woman, infant and suckling, ox and sheep,
camel and ass.

Each memory spawns ten.

In Sainsbury's Supermarket, a shrunken old man,
straggled beard – Jewish, surely – and his tiny wife,

too much lipstick – ponder over which pesto to try.
I help select a good brand, if a bit pricey. We talk

about sauce. We talk about English weather,
about teenagers suddenly with knives

Suddenly, I see the two of them,
holding hands, walking along a cobbled street,

too slow for the men in boots, guns and thumbs
in their belts. Turn away, I tell myself,

before they see me cry. I am
my own Job's comforter.

A Tailor's Song

I had a woollen coat, a hand-me-down from papa.
Already worn, torn and patched, it let in winter air,

so what was the use? I made it into a jacket but soon
the threads unravelled – worn, torn, so what was the use?

I tried it as a vest – but without buttons, all wrong.
The vest became a bag but my keys kept falling through,

so what was the use? I tore it into rags to polish silver,
and when they got too black, it was time to give up the coat.

Now nothing's of use to me, except this little song.

SOURCES, TRANSLITERATIONS, LITERAL TRANSLATIONS AND LINKS TO MUSIC*

.

BASHERTE

A re-imagination of the folksong *A Khosn On A Kale* ('A Groom Without a Bride'), words by Leyb Kvitko (1890-1952), music by Joseph Shrogin (n.d.), also attributed to Emil Gorovets (1923-2001). Transliteration and literal translation by Hélène Katz at http://rama01.free.fr/yidlid/chansons/khosn-on-kale.htm. MP3 version of the song by Hilda Bronstein may be purchased at http://www.amazon.co.uk/gp/product/B003W64P6E?ie=UTF8&ref=oce_digital.

Zaynen mir aroysgeforn
Oyfn ershtn shlitn,
Ale mekhuteneste,
Di kale in der mitn.
Oy, oy, zingen ale,
Nor es shvaygt aleyn di kale
Oy, oy, oy.

Zaynen mir aroysgeforn
Oyfn tsveytn shlitn,
Ale mekhutonim,
Der khosn in der mitn.
Oy, oy, zingen ale,
Nor es shvaygt aleyn di kale
Oy, oy, oy.

Zaynen mir aroysgeforn
Oyfn dritn shlitn,
Kales tsad un khosns tsad,

59

Di klezmer in der mitn.
Oy, oy, shpiln ale,
Vos zhe shvaygt di kale?
Oy, oy, oy.

Vi mir zaynen aroysgeforn,
Flit farbay a rayter.
Hot di kale oyfgeflamt,
Vi a fayer shayter.
Oy, oy, shvaygn ale,
Nor es zingt aleyn di kale
Oy, oy, oy.

Shlitelekh, ir shlitelekh,
It megt tsurik shoyn forn.
Khosn-lebn, oy, khosn-lebn,
Azvey tsu dayne yorn!
Oy, oy, okhtsen ale,
Zen a khosn on a kale
Oy, oy, oy.

We went out
On the first sled,
All the family's women,
The bride in the middle.
Oh, oh, everyone sings,
Only the bride is silent
Oh, oh, oh.

We went out
On the second sled,
All the family's men,
The groom in the middle.
Oh, oh, everyone sings,
Only the bride is silent
Oh, oh, oh.

We went out
On the third sled,
The bride's side, and the groom's side,
The musicians in the middle.
Oh, oh, they all played,
So why is the bride alone silent?
Oh, oh, oh.

As we went out,
Flew past us a [Polish] knight.
The bride flared up,
As a flaming bonfire.
Oh, oh, everyone's silent,
Only the bride sings
Oh, oh, oh.

Little sleds, little sleds,
You may go back already.
Bridegroom, oh bridegroom,
Woe is on your years!

Oh, everyone moans,
See: a groom without a bride
Oh, oh, oh.

CAVE SONG

A re-imagination of the poem in Yiddish, *Zog Maran* ('Say,
Marrano') by Abraham Reisen (1876-1953), set to song by Samuel
Bugatch (1898-1984). Yiddish lyrics from Eleanor Gordon Mlotek
and Joseph Mlotek, *Pearls of Yiddish Song,* New York: Workmen's
Circle, 1988, p. 205. Translation by the Mloteks. The song may be
heard at http://www.youtube.com/watch?v=aF5fxWBXr0w.

– Zog maran, du bruder mayner,
Vu iz greyt der seyder dayner?
– In tifr heyl in a kheyder,
dort hob ikh gegreyt mayn seyder.

– Zog maran mir vu bay vemen
Vestu vayse matzos nemen?
– In der heyl oyf Gots barotn,
Hot mayn vayb dem teyg geknotn.

– Zog maran vi vest zikh klign
A hagode vu tsu krign?
– In der heyl, in tife shpaltn,
Hob ikh zi shoyn lang bahaltn.

– Zog maran, vi vest zikh vern
Ven men vet dayn kol derhern?
– Ven der soyne vet mikh fangen,
Vel ikh shtarbn mit gezangen.

Tell me, Marrano, my brother,
Where are you preparing your seder?
– In a deep cave, in a hollow,
There I prepared my seder.

Tell me, Marrano, from whom
Will you get white *matsos*?
– In the cave, at the mercy of God,
My wife kneaded the flour.

Tell me, Marrano, how will you rack your brain
To get yourself a *haggadah*?
– In the cave, in deep recesses,
I've been hiding it for a long time.

Tell me, Marrano, how will you defend yourself
If someone hears your voice?
– If the enemy captures me,
I will die singing.

TEN BROTHERS

A re-imagination of traditional lyrics set to music by Abraham Ell-
stein (1907-1963). The song in modern tempo can be heard on Wolf

63

Krakowski's CD, *Transmigrations: Gilgul*. Transliteration and literal translation Wolf Krakowski and Fraidy Katzat, © Kame'a Media 1996, at http://www.kamea.com/tmlyrics.pdf. See also Alex Lubet: *Transmigrations: Wolf Krakowski's Yiddish Worldbeat in its Socio-Musical Context*, in: *Polin: Studies in Polish Jewry*, vol. 16, *Jewish Popular Culture and its Afterlife*. Edited by Michael C. Steinlauf and Antony Polonsky, 2003, pp 297-312: '*Tsen Brider* ('Ten Brothers')... a pitifully bitter lyric, counts backwards as each brother dies until only one remains'. A grimmer ending came out of the Sachsenhausen concentration camp. 'Lenin...' is an anonymous alternative to *Yidl mitn fidl...: Lenin mitn fidl/ Trotstki mitn bas/Zingen zey a lidl/ Za rabokhi klas* (http://zemerl.com/cgi-bin//show.pl?title=Leni n+mit+dem+fidl%2c+Trotsky+mot+dem+bas). A fine rendition by André Heller, accompanied by wonderful photos of Jewish pedlars and workmen in Eastern Europe, may be heard at http://www.youtube.com/watch?v=P-q_p4zQmro.

Tsen brider zenen mir gevezn,
Hobn mir gehandlt mit vayn.
Eyner fun undz iz undz geshtorbn,
Zenen mir geblibn nayn.
Nayn brider zenen mir gevezn,
Hobn mir gehandlt mit frakht.

Eyner fun undz iz geshtorbn,
Zenen mir geblibn akht.

Refren:
Yidl mitn fidl, Gedalye mitn bas,
Shpil-zhe mir a lidl oyfn mitn gas.

Akht brider zenen mir gevezn,
Hobn mir gehandlt mit ribn.
Eyner fun undz iz geshtorbn,
Zenen mir geblibn zibn.
Zibn brider zenen mir gevezn,
Hobn mir gehandlt mit gebeks.
Eyner fun undz iz geshtorbn,
Zenen mir geblibn zeks.

Ref...

Zeks brider zenen mir gevezn,
Hobn mir gehandlt mit shtrimp.
Eyner fun undz iz geshtorbn,
Zenen mir geblibn finf.
Finf brider zenen mir gevezn,
Hobn mir gehandlt mit bir.
Eyner fun undz iz geshtorbn,
Zenen mir geblibn fir.

Ref...

Fir brider zenen mir gevezn,
Hobn mir gehandlt mit blay.
Eyner fun undz iz geshtorbn,
Zenen mir geblibn dray.
Dray brider zenen mir gevezn,
Hobn mir gehandlt mit tey.
Eyner fun undz iz geshtorbn,
Zenen mir geblibn tsvey.

Ref...

Tsvey brider zenen mir gevezn,
Hobn mir gehandlt mit beyner.
Eyner fun undz iz geshtorbn,
Bin ikh mir geblibn nor eyner.
Eyn bruder bin ikh mir geblibn,
Handl ikh mit likht.
Shtarbn tu ikh yedn tog
Vayl tsu esn hob ikh nisht.

Ref...

We were ten brothers,
We dealt in wine.
One of us died,
Nine of us remained.
We were nine brothers,
We dealt in freight.
One of us died,
Eight of us remained.

Refrain:
Yidl with your fiddle, Gedalye with your bass,
Play a little tune in the middle of the street.

We were eight brothers,
We dealt in turnips.
One of us died,
Seven of us remained.

We were seven brothers,
We dealt in baked goods.
One of us died,
Six of us remained.

Ref...

We were six brothers,
We dealt in hose.
One of us died,
Five of us remained.
We were five brothers,
We dealt in beer.
One of us died,
Four of us remained.

Ref...

We were four brothers,
We dealt in lead.
One of us died,
Three of us remained.

We were three brothers,
We dealt in tea.
One of us died,
Two of us remained.

Ref...

We were two brothers,
We dealt in bones.
One of us died,
I am left alone.
I remain the only brother,
I deal in candles.
I die every day
Because I have nothing to eat.

Ref...

MAKE A LIVING

A re-imagination of the Yiddish folksong, *Bin Ikh Mir a Shnayderl*
('I'm a Little Tailor'), author unknown. Literal translation found
at: http://zemerl.com/cgi-bin//print.pl?title=Bin+Ikh+Mir+a+Shnayderl,
supplemented by Norbert Hirschhorn. The song can be bought at
http://www.myspace.com/schmittskatzen/music/songs/bin-ikh-mir-
a-shnayderl-64655577.

Bin ikh mir a shnayderl
Leb ikh mir tog oys tog ayn
Lustik, freylekh, fayn!
– Zog mir, shnayderl, libinker un guter
Git dir di nodl genug oyf broyt un puter?
– Ikh makh a vokh tsvey gildn mit a drayer
Ikh es nor broyt vayl puter iz tsu tayer.

Bin ikh mir a shusterl
Leb ikh mir tog oys tog ayn
Lustik, freylekh, fayn!
– Zog mir, shusterl, hostu vos tsu kayen?
Felt dir oyset krigstu vu tsu layen?
– Keyner layt nisht, keyner git keyn orves,
Ikh bin a shuster, gey ikh take borves.

Bin ikh mir a kremerl,
Leb ikh mir tog oys tog ayn
Lustik, freylekh, fayn!
– Zog mir kremerl, host mit vos tsu handlen?
Host in kreml rozhinkes mit mandlen?
– Ikh hob in kreml far tsvey groshn skhoyre
Ikh shlep dem dales un ikh bentsh dem Boyre.

I'm a little tailor,
I live from day to day,
Cheerfully, joyfully and fine!
– Tell me, good little tailor
Does your needle bring you bread and butter?
– I earn two small coins and another penny,
Enough to buy some bread, but butter too dear.

I'm a little cobbler,
I live from day to day
Cheerfully, joyfully and fine!
– Tell me, little cobbler, what have you to eat?
If you are lacking, can you borrow somewhere?

– No one lends, no one gives loan guaranty.
I'm a cobbler, I go barefoot.

I'm a little shopkeeper,
I live from day to day,
Cheerfully, joyfully and fine!
– Tell me shopkeeper, have you wares to deal in?
Have you raisins and almonds in your shop?
– In my shop I have two penny worth of goods.
I drag around my poverty and bless the Creator.

THREE SISTERS

A re-imagination of the song *Dray Shvester* ('Three Sisters') by
Morris Winchevsky (1856-1932); transliteration and literal transla-
tion from Metropolitan Klezmer CD 'Surprising Finds', 2002.

In England iz do a shtot Lester,
Un in London iz do aza skver.
In skver shteyen teglekh dray shvester,
Di meydlekh, zey ken ver-nit-ver.

Di kleynste farkoyft dortn blumen,
Di mitelste bendlekh fun shikh,
Un shpet in der nakht zet men kumen
Di elste, vos handlt mit zikh.

Di yingere beyde batrakhtn
Di eltere shvester on has;

70

Vayl ale dray shvester farakhtn
Di velt, mit der shot, mit der gas.

Un dokh, ven di kleyne tsvey kumen
Tsum nest, vos zey rufn 'a heym',
Banetsn zey bendlekh un blumen
Mit trern, vos blaybn geheym.

In England is a town called Leicester,
And in London there is such a square.
In this square three sisters stand every day,
The girls, someone or other will know them.

The youngest sells flowers there,
The middle girl, shoe laces and bows,
And late at night you can see
The eldest one who sells herself.

The two younger ones both regard
Their older sister without hate;
Because all three sisters look with contempt
On the world, and the city, and the street.

And yet when the two youngest come back
To the nest they call 'home',
They moisten the flowers and shoelaces
With tears that stay private.

THE LITTLE STOVE

A re-imagination of the classic Yiddish song, *Oyfn Pripetshik*
('Atop the Stove') by Mark Warshavsky (1840-1907). Lyrics and
music can be found at http://www.ibiblio.org/yiddish/songs/prip-
etshek/; a boys' choir sings the song at http://www.youtube.com/
watch?v=JkS3cZntDTY. Literal translation by Norbert Hirschhorn.

Oyfn pripetshik brent a fayerl,
Un in shtub iz heys.
Un der rebe lernt kleyne kinderlekh
Dem alef-beyz.

Refren:
Zet zhe, kinderlekh, gedenkt zhe, tayere,
Vos ir lernt do,
Zogt zhe nokh a mol un take nokh a mol:
Komets-alef: *O!*

Lernt, kinder, hot nit moyre,
Yeder onheyb is shver,
Gliklekh der, vos hot gilernt toyre,
Tsi darf a mentsh nokh mer?

Ref:

Lernt, kinder, mit groys kheyshek,
Azoy zog ikh aykh on,
Ver s'vet gikher fun aykh kenen ivre,
Der bakumt a fon.

Ref:

Az ir vet, kinder, elter vern,
Vet ir aleyn farshteyn,
Vifl in di oysyes lign trern
In vifl geveyn.

Ref:

Az ir vet, kinder, dem goles shlepn,
Oysgemutshet zayn,
Zolt ir fun di oysyes koyekh shepn,
Kukt in zey arayn!

Ref:

On the stove a little fire is burning,
And it is hot in the house.
And the rebbe is teaching little children
The A B Cs.

Refrain:
See now children, remember dear ones,
What you're learning here;
Say it again and even again:
Aleph with a 'komets' sign is *O!*

Study, children, don't be afraid,
Every beginning is difficult.

73

Happy he who learns the Torah,
Does a person need more?

Ref:

Learn, children, with great eagerness,
This is what I tell you:
Who is the fastest of you to learn Hebrew
He receives a flag.

Ref:

As you, children, get older,
You will yourselves understand,
How many tears lie in these letters
And how much weeping.

Ref:

As you, children, haul the burden of exile,
Become exhausted,
You will derive strength from these letters
So look into them!

Ref:

Jump Rope Songs

I

A re-imagination based on a skipping rhyme used by Jewish children in Eastern Europe. Source: *Mendele Moykher-Sforim* – S.Y. Abramovich – cited and with literal translation by Ruth Rubin, *Voices of a People. The Story of Yiddish Folksong,* Urbana and Chicago: University of Illinois Press, 2000, p. 48.

A zun mit a regn, di kale iz gelegn,
Vos hot zi gehat? – A yingele.
Vi azoy hot es geheysn? – Moyshele.
Vu hot men es gevigt? – In a vigele.
Vu hot men es bagrobn? – In a gribele.

II

A re-imagination of an anonymous children's song ('reflecting the environment into which they had been born') from Ruth Rubin, *Voices of a People. The Story of Yiddish Folksong,* Urbana and Chicago: University of Illinois Press, 2000, p. 280. Literal translation by Rubin.

Oy vey muter,
Di kats lekt di puter,
Di hiner leygn di eyer,
Di kale geyt in shleyer,
Der khosn geyt in tales,
Baym kabtsn iz der dales,
Di kinder zoygn di finger,
Di vayber shtarbn far hunger.

I

Sun and rain, the bride had a baby,
What did she have? – A little boy.
What did she call him? – Moyshele.
Where was he rocked? – In a cradle.
Where was he buried? – In a little grave.

II

Oh, oh, mother
The cat's licking the butter,
The hens are laying eggs,
The bride wears the veil,
The groom wears the prayer shawl,
The poor man has his poverty,
The children suck their fingers,
The women die of hunger.

FROM MY MOUTH

A re-imagination of the song *Rozhinkes Mit Mandlen* ('Raisins with
Almonds'), one of the best beloved of Yiddish folksongs, written by
Abraham Goldfaden (1840-1906) for his operetta, Shulamis, based
on a traditional song, *Unter Yankeles Vigele*. Goldfaden was the
founder of modern Yiddish theater. Published in Eleanor Gordon
Mlotek, *Mir Trogen a Gezang! Favorite Yiddish Songs of Our
Generation*. Third edition, New York: Workman's Circle, 1972, p.
4. Literal translation by Norbert Hirschhorn. There are several ver-

sions of lyrics to this song; here is a beautiful rendition, if truncated:
http://www.youtube.com/watch?v=YdKkPupLiYM.

In dem beys-hamikdesh,
In a vinkl kheyder,
Zitst di almone, Bas-Tsiyen aleyn.

Ir ben-yokhidl Yidelen vigt zi keseyder
Un zingt im tsum shlofn a lidele sheyn:

Unter Yideles vigele
Shteyt a klor-vays tsigele,
Dos tsigele is geforn handlen,
Dos vet zayn dayn baruf:
Rozhinkes mit mandlen,
Shlof zhe, Yidele, shlof.

Es vert kumen a tsayt fun ayznbanen,
Zey veln farfleytsen a halbe velt;
Ayzerne vegn vestu oysshpanen,
Un vest in dem oykh fardinen fil gelt.

Un az du vest vern raykh, Yidele,
Zolstu zikh dermonen in dem lidele,
Rozhinkes mit mandlen!
Dos vet zayn dayn baruf
Yidele vet alts handlen,
Shlof zhe, Yidele, shlof.

In the temple,
In the corner of a chamber

77

Sits a widow, Daughter of Zion, alone.
As she rocks her only son Yidele to sleep,
She sings him a pretty song, a lullaby:

Under Yidele's cradle
There stands a snow-white kid.
The kid has been to market,
It will be your calling, too:
Trading in raisins and almonds,
And now sleep, Yidele, sleep.

There will come a time when railroads
Will flood half the world.
You'll travel those iron roads,
And you will earn much money.

When you grow rich, Yidele,
You will recall this pretty song,
Raisins with Almonds!
It will be your calling,
Yidele will be trading in all wares.
Sleep, then, Yidele, sleep.

FROM PODWOLOCZYSKA TO ELLIS ISLAND

A re-imagination of the traditional folksong, *Her Nor, Du Sheyn Meydele* ('Listen, Pretty Girl'), set to music, transliteration and literal translation in Wolf Krakowski's CD *Transmigrations: Gilgul* – Kame'a Media: http://www.kamea.com/tmlyrics.pdf

('booklet'). Hear another rendition at http://www.youtube.com/
watch?v=PP0oXcF9oDA.

Her nor, du sheyn meydele,
Her nor, du fayn meydele,
Vos vestu ton in aza vaytn veg?

Ikh vel geyn in ale gasn
Un vel shrayen: vesh tsum vashn!
Abi mit dir tsuzamen zayn.

Her nor, du sheyn meydele,
Her nor, du fayn meydele,
Vu vestu vashn in aza vaytn veg?

Du vest meynen, az ikh bin shvakh –
Ikh ken vashn in dem taykh,
Abi mit dir tsuzamen zayn.

Her nor, du sheyn meydele,
Her nor, du fayn meydele,
Vos vestu esn in aza vaytn veg?

Broyt mit zalts vel ikh esn,
Tate-mame vel ikh fargesen
Abi mit dir tsuzamen zayn.

Her nor, du sheyn meydele,
Her nor, du fayn meydele,
Af vos vestu shlofn in aza vaytn veg?

Ikh bin nokh a yunge froy,
Ikh ken shlofn af a bintl shtroy
Abi mit dir tsuzamen zayn.

Her nor, du sheyn meydele,
Her nor, du fayn meydele,
Mit vos vestu zikh tsudekn in aza vaytn veg?

Der toy fun himl vet mikh tsudekn,
Di feygelekh veln mikh oyfvekn,
Abi mit dir tsuzamen zayn.

Listen, pretty girl,
Listen, you fine girl,
What will you do on such a long journey?

I will go through every street
And shout, 'I wash clothes!'
As long as I can be with you.

Listen, pretty girl,
Listen, you fine girl,
Where will you wash on such a long journey?

Do you think I'm weak?
I can do the wash in the river
As long as I can be with you.

Listen, pretty girl,
Listen, you fine girl,
What will you eat on such a long journey?

I will eat bread and salt,
I will forsake my parents,
As long as I can be with you.

Listen, pretty girl,
Listen, you fine girl,
Where will you sleep on such a long journey?

I'm still a young woman,
I can sleep on a bundle of straw
As long as I can be with you.

Listen, pretty girl,
Listen, you fine girl,
What for a cover on such a long journey?

Dew from the skies will cover me,
The birds will awaken me,
As long as I can be with you.

MY COUSIN THE GREENHORN

A re-imagination of a popular Yiddish song, *Di Grine Kuzine* ('The Greenhorn Cousin'), music by Abraham Schwartz (1881-1963), lyrics by Hyman Prizant; a perennial favorite for Klezmorim.

Listen to a sedate version of the song at http://uk.youtube.com/ watch?v=ndY1Hc3xa8c and the Klezmer one at http://uk.youtube. com/watch?v=vNpasfW0dmY&feature=related. Published in Eleanor Gordon Mlotek, *Mir Trogen a Gezang! Favorite Yiddish Songs of Our Generation*. Third edition, New York: Workman's Circle, 1972, p. 142. Literal translation found at http://zemerl.com/ cgi-bin//show.pl?title=Di+Grine+Kusine, supplemented by Norbert Hirschhorn.

Es iz su mir gekumen a kuzine
Sheyn vi gold iz zi geven, di grine,
Bekelekh vi royte pomerantsn
Fiselekh vos betn zikh tsum tantsn.

Herelekh vi zaydn-veb gelokte
Tseyndelekh vi perelekh getokte,
Eygelekh vi himl-bloy in friling
Lipelekh vi karshelekh a tsviling.

Nit gegangen iz zi – nor geshprungen,
Nisht geredt hot zi, nor gezungen;
Freylekh, lustik iz geven ir mine
Ot aza geven iz mayn kuzine!

Un azoy ariber zenen yorn,
Fun mayn kuzine iz a tel gevorn
'Peydeys' hot zi yorn lang geklibn
Biz fun ir iz gornisht nit geblibn.

Haynt az ikh bagegn mayn kuzine,
Un ikh freg zi: Vos zhe makhtsu, grine?
Entfernt zi mir mit a krumer mine:
Brenen zol Kolombuses medine!

A girl cousin arrived, a greenhorn.
Beautiful as gold she was,
Cheeks red as oranges,
Tiny feet, just made for dancing.

Her hair was as a silk web,
Her teeth as pearls on a string,
Her eyes, blue as skies in spring,
Her lips, just like twin cherries.

She did not walk, she leapt.
She did not talk, she sang.
Her every feature joyful and gay –
Such a one was my cousin!

But, as the years passed by
My cousin became a wreck
Collecting 'pay days' for years
Until nothing remained of her.

Today, as I meet her on the street,
And I ask: How's everything, Greenhorn?
She replies with a sour look:
To hell with Columbus's paradise!

MAYN RUE-PLATS

A re-imagination of the Yiddish song, *Mayn Rue-Plats* ('My Resting Place') written by Morris Rosenfeld (1862-1923) in response to the New York Triangle Shirtwaist Factory fire in 1911 when over 130 young immigrant women were killed as they jumped to escape the flames, the exits having been locked. Literal translation by anonymous: http://zemerl.com/cgi-bin//show.pl?title=Mayn+Rue+Platz. A heart-stop rendition may be heard at http://www.youtube.com/watch?v=tJkBGa3dxQM.

Nit zukh mikh, vu di mirtn grinen,
Gefinst mikh dortn nit, mayn shats.
Vu lebns velkn bay mashinen,
Dortn iz mayn rue-plats.

Nit zukh mikh, vu die feygl zingen,
Gefinst mikh dortn nit, mayn shats.
A shklaf bin ikh, vu keytn klingen,
Dortn iz mayn rue-plats.

Nit zukh mikh, vu fontanen shpritsn,
Gefinst mikh dortn nit, mayn shats.
Vu trern rinen, tseyner kritsn,
Dortn iz mayn rue-plats.

Un libst du mikh mit varer libe,
To kum tsu mir, mayn guter shats.
Un hayter oyf mayn harts, dos tribe,
Un makh mir zis mayn rue-plats.

Don't look for me where myrtles are green,
You will not find me there, my beloved.
Where lives wither at the machines,
There is my resting place.

Don't look for me where birds sing,
You will not find me there, my beloved.
I am a slave, where chains ring;
There is my resting place.

Don't look for me where fountains spray,
You will not find me there, my beloved.
Where tears flow and teeth gnash,
There is my resting place.

And if you love me with true love,
So come to me, my good beloved,
And lighten up my heavy heart,
And make sweet my resting place.

ABECEDARIAN FOR THE WORKERS OF THE WORLD

A re-imagination of a traditional acrostic song, *Alef-Indikes* ('A is for Turkey'). Eleanor and Joseph Mlotek, *Songs of Generations. New Pearls of Yiddish Song*, New York: Workmen's Circle, 2004, p. 67. Literal translation by the Mloteks as modified by Norbert Hirschhorn.

Alef – indikes est der nogid,
Beyz – beyndelekh grizhet der oreman.

Giml – gendzelekh est der nogid,
Daled – dem dales hot der oreman.

Hey – hindelekh gepreglte est der nogid,
Vov – veytikn hot der oreman.

Zayen – zeml mit puter est der nogid,
Khes – khaloshes hot der oreman.

Tes – taybelekh gebrotene est der nogid,
Yud – yesurim hot der oreman.

Kof – kalozhn trogt der nogid,
Lamed – laptshes trogt der oreman.

Mem – mashke trinkt der nogid,
Nun – nikhter iz der oreman.

Samekh – sametene kleyder trogt der nogid,
Ayen – opgerisn geyt der oreman.

Pey – pupkes est der nogid,
Tsadik – tsores hot der oreman.

Kuf – kotletn gepreglte est der nogid,
Reysh – retekh grizhet der oreman.

Shin – Shereshevskis* papirosn reykhert der nogid,
Tof – tutin pipket der oreman.

A cigarette factory in Grodno, Poland.

The rich man eats turkey
The poor man gnaws bones

The rich man eats goose
The poor man eats in squalor

The rich man has fried chicken
The poor man has aches and pains

The rich man eats rolls with butter
The poor man has nausea

The rich man eats roast pigeons
The poor man has suffering

The rich man wears galoshes
The poor man wears straw shoes

The rich man drinks whiskey
The poor man's a teetotaler

The rich man wears velvet clothes
The poor man wears rags

The rich man eats gizzards
The poor man has sorrows

The rich man dines on fried chops
The poor man gnaws on radishes

The rich man smokes cigarettes
The poor man puffs on weeds

A PUNTER'S LAMENT

A re-imagination of a raucous folk song, *Dem Ganevs Yikhes*
('The Thief's Pedigree'), also known as *Far Vos Bistu Ketsele
Broyges* ('Why are You Angry, Pussycat?'); source unknown.
Anonymous literal translation at http://zemerl.com/cgi-bin//show.
pl?title=Dem+Ganef4s+Yikhes+-+Far+Vos+Du+Ketsele+Broyges.
The song with other lyrics may be heard at http://www.youtube.com/
watch?v=GtcoSxtCBqo.

Vos-zhe bistu, ketsele broyges,
Vos geystu aropgelozt di noz?
Oy, efsher vilstu visn dayn yikhes,
Ken ikh dir zogn ver un vos ...
Dayn tate iz a shmarovoznik,
Dayn mame ganvet fish in mark,
Un dayn bruder iz a kartyozhnik,
Un dayn shvester geyt mit a soldat
Dayn feter iz geshtanen oyf di rogn,
Dayn mume – a hendlerke in mark,

Un dayn bruder zitst in di ostrogn,
Un dayn shvester geyt mit a matros.
Dayn zeyde iz geven a shoykhet,
Dayn bobe a tukerin in bod,
Un aleyn bistu, oy, a mamzer,
Un genumen bistu fun priut.

Why, little kitten, are you so angry?
Why is your nose turned down?
Oh, perhaps you'd like to know your breeding?
I can tell you who and what...
Your father greases wagon wheels,
Your mother steals fish at the fair,
And your brother is a card-sharp,
And your sister lives with a Cossack.

Your uncle hangs around streetcorners,
Your aunt a street-peddler,
And your brother sits in prison,
And your sister goes with a sailor.

Your grandpa was a ritual slaughterer,
Your grandma a bath-house attendant,
And you yourself are a bastard,
Taken from an orphanage.

A CZARIST CONSCRIPT BIDS FAREWELL

A re-imagination of the folksong, *Zayt Gezunt* ('Be Well'), by S.
Ginsburg and P. Marek (1901). From *Yidishe Folkslider* compiled by
M. Beregovsky and A. Fefer, Kiev, USSR: *Melukhe Farlag,* 1938,

89

p. 265. Reproduced digitally by National Yiddish Book Center, Amherst, MA. Literal translation by Norbert Hirschhorn. In that archive the song was a bride's farewell to her parents; but the second stanza is also found in a conscript's farewell to his parents. For a description of conscription of Jews under the Czars see http://grossmanproject.net/Military%20Conscription.htm.

A zayt gezunt, mayne libe eltern!
Kh'for avek in a vaytn veg,
Vu keyn vint veyt nit,
Un vu keyn feygele flit nit,
Un vu keyn hon kreyt nit.

Zayt gezunt, mayne libe eltern!
Ikh for fun aykh avek.
Got zol gebn
Gezunt un lebn,
Un mir a gliklekhn veg!

Good health to you, my dear parents!
I travel away on a distant road,
To where no wind blows,
And where no little bird sings,
And where no rooster crows.

Good health to you, my dear parents!
I travel far away from you.
God should give
Health and life,
And to me a fortunate way!

90

THE HAPPY CONSCRIPT

A re-imagination of the several-versioned song, *Yosl Ber*, original words by Itsik Manger (1901-1969). Here a composite from Eleanor Gordon Mlotek and Joseph Mlotek, *Pearls of Yiddish Song*, New York: Workmen's Circle, 1988, p. 173; and in parentheses from http://www.lyricsvip.com/Daniel-Kahn-%26-The-Painted-Bird/Yosl-Ber-/-A-Patriot-Lyrics.html. Literal translation by Norbert Hirschhorn. The song is better delivered raucously: http://www.youtube.com/watch?v=KyKn7n-0e7E; but here more sedately: http://www.youtube.com/watch?v=BGZQPh4lW6M.

Heysn heys ikh Yosl-Ber
Un ikh din in militer –
Shtivl trog ikh, a mundir,
Lehavdl vi an ofitsir.

(Yosl Ber
Dint in militer,
Yosl, Yosl, Yosl Ber
Dint in militer.)

Geven bin ikh a shuster-yung,
Gelekt podeshves mitn tsung –
Haynt hob ikh a biks, a shverd,
Shusteray hob ikh in dr'erd.

(*Vashe visokorodye,* kh'bin take a trayer
zelner un take derfar bin ikh antlofn!

Ikh hob azoy faynt dem soyne, az ikh vel
im afile in di oygn nit onkukn.)

Mit dem bezem iz mir gring,
Kh'ker kazarmes un ikh zing –
S'endikt zikh di bezem-shlakht,
Dank ikh Got, s'falt tsu nakht.

Gey ikh mir in gas aroys
Un ikh zukh a meydl oys –
Gib ikh zikh ir a boyg
Un a pintl mitn oyg.

Farbet zi mikh in kikh arayn,
Git mir bronfn, git mir vayn –
Zi git mir a bulke, fish un khreyn,
Oy, a meydl mole-kheyn.

(Yosl Ber
Dint in militer,
Yosl, Yosl, Yosl Ber
Dint in militer.)

My name is Yosl Ber
And I serve in the army –
I wear boots and a uniform,
Pardon the expression, like an officer.

(Yosl Ber
serves in the army

Yosl, Yosl, Yosl Ber
serves in the army.)

I was an apprentice cobbler,
Licking soles with my tongue –
Now I have a rifle, a sword,
Cobbling can go to hell.

(Your Honour, I'm indeed a faithful
Soldier, that's why I ran away!
I hate the enemy so much that
I wouldn't even look him in the eye.)

With the broom I take it easy,
Sweep the barracks while I sing –
As the broom-combat ends,
I thank God that night falls.

I go out in the street
And I pick up a girl –
I give her a bow
And a wink.

She invites me into the kitchen,
Gives me whiskey, gives me wine –
She gives a roll, fish and horse radish,
Oh, what a flirty girl.

(Yosl Ber

Serves in the army

Yosl, Yosl, Yosl Ber

Serves in the army.)

SCAPEGOATS

A re-imagination of *Dos Kelbl* ('The Little Calf'), also known as *Dona, Dona*; a metaphor for the inevitability of Jewish suffering and the world's complicity or indifference. Text by A. Zeitlin, music by Sholem Sekunda. Literal translation in A. Vinkovetzky, A. Kovner, S. Leichter, *Anthology of Yiddish Folksongs*, Second Edition, Vol. 4, Jerusalem: Hebrew University, 1987, p. 45-6. Rendition by the duo, Zupfgeigenhansel, http://www.youtube.com/watch?v=nZN80LDku2A

Oyfn furl ligt dos kelbl,
Ligt gebundn mit a shtrik;
Hoykh in himl flit dos shvelbl,
Flit un dreyt zikh hin un krik.

Refren:
Lakht der vint in korn,
Lakht un lakht un lakht,
Lakht er op a tog a ganstn
Mit a halber nakht...
Hey, dona-dona-dona!

Shrayt dos kelbl, zogt der poyer:
– Ver zhe heyst dir zayn a kalb?
Volst gekert tsu zayn a foygl,
Volst gekert tsu zayn a shvalb…

Ref:

Bidne kelblekh tut men bindn
Un me shlept zey un me shekht;
Ver s'hot fligl, flit aroyftsu
Iz bay keynem nit keyn knekht…

Ref:

Upon a wagon lies a calf –
Trussed up tightly it cannot stir.
High above there flies a swallow
Flying freely here and there.

Refrain:
Laughs the wind in the fields of corn,
Laughs with great delight.
It laughs and laughs throughout the day
And halfway through the night.
Hey, dona, dona, dona!

The little calf bleats, but says the farmer,
Who ever asked you to be a calf?
Were you born to be a bird
Like a swallow you'd be free.

Ref:

Poor little calves are tied and tethered
Dragged towards their bitter end.
But had you wings you would be free
And be no slave to anyone.

Ref:

A YIDDISHE MAMA LAMENTS

A response to the classic paean to all Jewish mothers, *Mayn Yidishe Mame,* sung by the famous cantor Yosef Rosenblatt (1882-1933), http://uk.youtube.com/watch?v=ZWWc7vBnSP0. Yiddish text at http://zemerl.com/cgi-bin//show.pl?title=My+Yiddishe+Mame, literal translation by Norbert Hirschhorn:

Ikh vil bay aykh a kashe fregn, zogt mir ver es ken:
Mit velkhe tayere farmegns bentsht Got alemen?
Men koyft es nit far keyn shtum gelt, dos git men nor umzist.
Un dokh az men farlirt dos, vifil trern men fargist.
A tsveyte git men keynem nit, es helft nit keyn geveyn,
Oy! Ver es hot farloyrn, der veys shoyn vos ikh meyn.
A yidishe mame, nito keyn besers oyf der velt.
A yidishe mame, oy vey, vi biter ven zi felt!
Vi sheyn un likhtik iz in hoyz, ven di mame iz do
Vi troyerik, fintster vert ven Got nemt ir oyf oylem-habo.
In vaser un fayer volt si gelofn far ir kind.
Nit haltn ir tayer, dos is gevis di greste zind.

Oy, vi gliklekh un raykh iz der mentsh, vos hot
Aza sheyne matone geshenkt fun Got,
Nor an altitshke yidishe mame,
Mame mayn.

I would like to ask a question, tell me whoever knows:
With what precious possession does God bless everyone?
Something one can't buy for any money, it only comes for free;
But if you lose it, what tears flow.
A second one is never given, it wouldn't help to weep,
Oh! Whoever has lost it, he knows well what I mean.
A yiddishe mama, nothing's better in the world.
A yiddishe mama, oy vey, how bitter when she's gone!
How lovely and light in the house when the mama is there;
How sad and dark when God takes her to the next world.

Through water and fire she'd run for her child.
Not to affirm her as the dearest is surely the greatest sin.
Oh, how lucky and rich is the person who has
Received this beautiful gift from God,
Simply a dear old yiddishe mama,
My mama.

A MARXIST LULLABY

A re-imagination of the Yiddish lullaby, *Shlof Mayn Kind, Shlof
Keseyder* ('Sleep My Child, Sleep Continuously'), lyrics by
Anonymous, put to music by Hugo Weisgall, 1912-1997. Literal
translation by Ruth Rubin in *Yiddish Folksongs from the Ruth Rubin*

Archive, edited by Chana Motel and Mark Slobin, Detroit: Wayne State University Press, 2007, p. 75.

Shlof mayn kind, shlof keseyder,
Zingen vel ikh dir a lid.
Az du mayn kind, vest elter vern,
Vestu visn an untershid.

Az du, mayn kind, vest elter vern,
Vestu vern mit laytn glaykh.
Demolst vestu gevoyre vern,
Vos heyst orem un vos heyst raykh.

Di tayerste palatsn, di shenste hayzer,
Dos alts makht der oreman,
Nor veystu ver es tut in zey voynen?
Gor nisht er, nor der raykher man.

Der oreman, er ligt in keler,
Der faykhtkeyt rint im fun di vent
Fun dem bakumt er a rematn-feler
In di fis un in di hent.

Sleep, my child, sleep,
I will sing you a song.
When you grow older,
You will understand the difference.

When you will grow older, my child,
You will be like the rest of us.

98

Then you will become aware,
What is poor and what is rich.

The most lavish palaces, loveliest mansions,
All are made by the poor man.
But do you know who lives in them?
Not he at all, but the rich man.

The poor man lies in the celler,
Dampness drips from the walls.
That is how he gets rheumatism
In his hands and in his feet.

SLEEP MY CHILD

A re-imagination blending two lullabies; one by Sholem Aleichem
(1859-1916), *Shlof Mayn Kind* ('Sleep My Child'); the other an unti-
tled response by Mitchell Kaplan (1881-1944); both lyrics and literal
translations from Ruth Rubin's *Voices of a People. The Story of
Yiddish Folksong,* Urbana and Chicago: University of Illinois Press,
2000; p. 40 and p. 362. A violinist's rendition of Sholem Aleichem's
song is at: http://www.youtube.com/watch?v=8YnsKnXE7Dg.

Sholem Aleichem

In Amerike iz der tate,
Dayner, zunenyu,
Du bist nokh a kind lesate,
Shlof-zhe, lyu-lyu-lyu.

Dortn est men in der vokhn
Khale, zunenyu,
Yaykhelekh vel ikh dir kokhn,

Shlof-zhe, lyu-lyu-lyu.

Er vet shikn tsvantsik doler,
Zayn portret dertsu,
Un vet nemen, lebn zol er!
Undz ahintsutsu.

Mitchell Kaplan

Ludlov Strit... bitere, voynungen,
    hoykhe,
Fintstere shtign a sakh...
Zunenyu, do voynt dayn tate, dayn
    oremer!
Opgetsert iz er un shvakh.

Tsedoke-kikh... tukhlekeyt...
    broyt alt-gebakns,...
Shitere, bitere yoykh...
Zunenyu, do est dayn tate, dayn
    oremer!
Klogt er zikh, shpayzt zikh mit
    roykh...

Glust er a shifskarte koyfn oyf
    oystsoln,

100

Klaybt zikh aheym shoyn fun
    lang…
Zunenyu, slek heyst a tsayt aza bitere,
Shtert dos dayn tatn in gang.

Sholem Aleichem

Your daddy's in America,
Your daddy, little son,
But you are still a child,
Sleep then, hushaby.

There they eat even on the weekdays
White bread, little son;
I will cook chicken broth there for you,

Sleep then, hushaby.

He will send us twenty dollars
And his picture, too,
And will take us – long life to him! –
To America.

Mitchell Kaplan

Ludlow St... dreary tall
    dwellings,
Many dark stairways there…
Dear son, here lives your poor

father!
Emaciated and weak is he.

Charity kitchen... putrid...
        stale bread,...
Watery, bitter soup...
Dear son, here your poor father
        eats!
Complaining he feeds on
        smoke...

He wants to buy a steamship ticket
        on payments,
Planning to return home for a long
        time now...
Dear son, such a bitter time is called 'slack'.
And it stands in your father's way.

A YIDDISH DIVORCE

A re-imagination of the folksong, *Tunkl Brent a Fayer* ('A Fire
Burns Dimly'), from Eleanor and Joseph Mlotek, *Songs of Genera-
tions. New Pearls of Yiddish Song*, New York: Workmen's Circle,
2004, p. 212. Literal translation by the Mloteks. The *get*, written in
Aramaic, is the instrument by which, with approval from a rab-
binical court, an orthodox Jew can divorce his wife, but with her
consent. The wording, *you are hereby permitted to all men,* is meant
to free both partners from the possibility of adultery.

Tunkl brent a fayer
In shtiln tsorn, blas,
An umet oyf der hayzl
An umet oyfn gas.

Der vint, der vint, der beyzer,
Er rayst mit beyz gefil;
Do klapt imer shtarker,
Do klapt imer shtil.

– Gut-ovnt, shvester Dvoyre,
Mayn kumen iz nisht gut.
Dayn man fun Amerike
Shikt dir op a get.

Er vil dikh nit kenen,
Er vil dikh nit visn;
Dayn man fun Amerike
Shikt dir op a get.

A fire burns dimly,
In silent rage, white.
Sorrow lies upon the house
And there is sorrow in the street.

The wind, the wind, the angry wind,
It tears at us with angry feeling;
Here it blows strongly,
Here it blows quietly.

Good evening, sister Deborah –
My coming is not good.
Your husband sends from America
A divorce for you.

He doesn't want to know you,
He doesn't want to acknowledge you.
Your husband from America
Is sending you a divorce.

THE LAST BRANCH PLEADS FOR RELEASE

A re-imagination of a Yiddish folksong *Vayl Ikh Bin a Tsvayg*
('Because I am a Branch'), by Beyle Schaechter-Gottesman (found
on her 2003 CD, *Af Di Gasn Fun Der Shtot*, available from Amazon;
transliteration and translation in the program notes). An alternative
version is at www.jewishfolksongs.com/vayl-ikh-bin-a-tsvayg.

Loz mir mayn kholem, shenk mir di ru.
Loz nor der vint farvign mayn sho.
Vayl ikh bin aleyn, an aleyniker tsvayg,
Der boym hot farloyrn zayn vortsl un shvaygt.

Un mir vilt zikh fort, aroyf afn boym,
Tsegrinen di bleter, tsetreyslen di kroyn,
Un mir glust zikh davke vi a foygl tsum nest
Tsuflien tsum shtam, zayn im a treyst!

Un vi a foygl kh'volt flien het hoykh,
Tselozn mayn kol s'zol, di khmares a durkh!
Un vi di pave fun altn lid,
Kh'vel zukhn di gildene feder vos flit.

Un plutsem derze ikh, tsi dakht zikh mir oys,
Se kumen on feygl, gor makhnesvays.
Mit groys geflater mit poyk un trumeyt,
Tsegrinen di bleter a simkhe, a freyd!

To loz mir mayn kholem, s'iz haynt mayn vor.
Me hot mikh farshribn vi dem letstn fun dor...
Nor ikh bin a tsvayg fun an altn boym
Un kh'vil se zol grinen un tsviten mayn kroyn!

Leave me my dream, send me rest.
Just let the wind rock my hour to sleep.
Because I am alone, a lonely branch,
The tree lost its root and is silent.

And still I feel like climbing the tree,
Greening the leaves, shaking the crown,
And I crave, just like a bird for its nest
To fly to the trunk and console it.

And like a bird, I'd fly up on high,
Let loose my voice to make it pierce the clouds!
And like the peacock from the old song,
I will seek the golden feather that flies.

And suddenly I see, or am I imagining it,
Birds arriving in large flocks.
With a great flutter, with drum and trumpet,
The leaves turn green, a celebration, a joy!

So leave me my dream, it's my reality now.
They've written me down as the last of my generation...
But I am a branch of an old tree, and
I want my crown to turn green and blossom!

THE NEIGHBOURING VILLAGE

A re-imagination of the song *Nakhtishe Lider* ('Night Time Songs')
originally a poem by Herz Rivkin (1908-1951) from his poetry
collection *In Shkheynishn Dorf* ('From the Neighbouring Village'),
Bucharest 1938, reprinted in Bucharest in 1977. Author of the
melody unknown. The transliteration, translation and song found at
http://yiddishsong.wordpress.com/2012/09/12/
nakhtishe-lider-performed-by-beyle-schaechter-gottesman.

Nakhtishe lider fun shkheynishn dorf
Farblondzhen amol tsu mayn ganik.
Zey leshn mayn troyer, zey gletn mayn umet.
Zey flisn vi zaftiger honik.

Lider ukraynishe, muntere, frishe,
Vos shmekn un mit feld un mit shayer.
Zey filn di luft mit varemkeyt liber,
Vos shtromt fun a heymishn fayer.

Nakht iz in shtetl, ikh lig afn ganik.
Ver darf haynt der mames geleger?
Iz vos, az s'iz eyns? Is vos, az s'iz tsvey?
Iz vos az s'shlogt dray shoyn der zeyger?

Her ikh un ikh veys nisht iz yontif in dorf.
Tsi es hulyen zikh glat azoy yungen.
Az vos iz der khilek? Oyb s'vet bald, mir dakht
di levone oykh onheybn tsu zingen.

Azoy gisn zikh fun shkheynishn dorf
heymishe zaftike tener.
Biz s'heybt on frimorgn tsu vargn di nakht
un es heybn on kreyen shoyn di hener.

Night songs from the neighbouring village
Lose their way to my porch.
They extinguish my sadness, they caress my melancholy;
They flow like juicy honey.

Ukrainian songs, upbeat and fresh
That smell of field and barn.
They fill the air with a loving warmth,
That streams from an intimate fire.

It's nighttime in town; I lie on my porch.
Who needs today my mother's place to sleep?
So what if it's one? So what if it's two?
So what if the clock strikes three?

I listen and don't know if it's a celebration in the village,
Or just some kids revelling.
But what is the difference? If soon, it seems
The moon will also start to sing.

In this way pours out, from the neighbouring village
Intimate, juicy melodies.
Until the early morning begins to choke the night
And the roosters start to crow.

ECCLESIASTES REDUX

A re-imagination of the Yiddish folk interpretation of Ecclesiastes
and its famous opening, 'Vanity of vanities' (King James Version).
Hevl in the original Hebrew actually connotes a breath, something
transient and of little substance. *Hevl* and the name Abel are cog-
nate. The literal translation comes from 'Yiddish Song of the Week',
July 2012, and as sung by Lilian Manuel. She is one of the elderly
persons whose memories of songs are recorded for posterity:
http://yiddishsong.wordpress.com/2012/07/06/
di-gantse-velt-iz-hevl-havolim-performed-by-lillian-manuel/.

Di gantse velt iz hevl-havolim,
Un di velt iz nor a kholem,
Un a kholem iz di velt,
Un zi shteyt dokh nor oyf gelt.

Un far gelt koyft men bir,
Un vos dray iz nit fir,

108

Un vos fir iz nit dray,
Un vos alt iz nit nay.

Un vos nay iz nit alt,
Un vos varem iz nit kalt,
Un vos kalt iz nit varem,
Un vos raykh iz nit orem.

Un vos orem iz nit raykh,
Un vos krum iz nit glaykh,
Un vos glaykh iz nit krum,
Un vos redt iz nit shtum.

The whole world is vanity of vanities,
And the world is just a dream,
And a dream is the world,
And it's constantly about money.

And for money one buys beer,
And three is not four,
And four is not three,
And what is old is not new.

And what is new is not old,
And what is warm is not cold,
And what is cold is not warm,
And what is rich, is not poor.

And what is poor is not rich,
And what is crooked is not straight,

And what is straight is not crooked,
And what is spoken is not mute.

FOR SURE

A re-imagination of *Der Tate iz Geforn* ('The Father Has Travelled'),
a mother-daughter dialogue, from Aharon Vinkovetzky, Abba
Kovner, Sinai Leichter, *Anthology of Yiddish Folksongs*, Volume
One, Jerusalem: Hebrew University Magnes Press, 1983, p. 40.
Literal translation by Norbert Hirschhorn. Note that *bayke* can mean
either a fine fabric, or a lie.

Der tate is geforn keyn Balte,
Hot er mir gebrakht a bayke,
Hot er mir gebrakht a bayke.

Ver vet dir neyen di bayke?
Sore di modistke, mame, dayke,
Ot zi vet mir neyen di bayke.

Un ven vestu onton di bayke?
Shabes nokhn kugl, mame, dayke,
Vel ikh onton di bayke.

Tsu vemen vestu geyn mit der bayke?
Tsu dem feter Yosl, mame, dayke,
Tsu im vel ikh geyn mit der bayke.

Mit vemen vestu zitsn in der bayke?
Mit zayn sheynem bokher, mama, dayke,
Mit im vel ikh zitsn in der bayke.

Vos vet zayn der sof fun der bayke?
Az er vet mikh nemen, mame, dayke, –
Ot dos vet zayn der sof fun der bayke.

Papa has travelled to Balta,
He bought me a fine fabric,
He bought me a fine fabric.

Who will tailor this fine fabric?
Sarah, the modiste, mama, for sure,
She will tailor this fine fabric.

And when will you put on this fine clothing?
After the Sabbath noodles, mama, for sure,
Then I'll put on the fine garment.

To whom will you go wearing this fine clothing?
To Uncle Yosl, mama, for sure,
To him I'll go wearing this fine clothing.

With whom will you sit in your fine clothing?
With his lovely son, mama, for sure,
I'll sit with him in my fine clothing.

What will come of this fine clothing?

He'll ask me to marry him, mama, for sure,

And that'll be the finish of this fine clothing.

THE WANDERING JEW

A re-imagination of a traditional folksong, *Ikh Nem Dos Pekl*
('I Take the Bundle') found on www.zemerl.com/cgi-bin//show.
pl?title=ikh+nem+dos+pekl; no attributions given. Literal transla-
tion by Norbert Hirschhorn.

Ikh nem dos pekl oyf den shtekl,

Oy, vos freg ikh aykh?

Un dos rentsl oyf di pleytses,

Yo, vos broykh ikh aykh?

Ikh hob a shtub un zibn kinder,

Oy, vos freg ikh aykh?

Un a tsig un zibn gildn,

Yo, vos broykh ikh aykh?

Un der regn klatsht in fentsterl,

Oy, vos freg ikh aykh?

Un der dales fayft in koymen,

Yo, vos broykh ikh aykh?

Oyfn hartsn iz keyn mut nit,

Oy, vos freg ikh aykh?

Ir fort tsum rebn, oy, tsum rebn,

Yo, vos broykh ikh aykh?

I take the bundle on a stick,
Oh, what can I ask of you?
And the satchel on the shoulders,
Yeah, what do I need you for?
I have a hut with seven children,
Oh, what can I ask of you?
And a goat and seven guilders,
Yeah, what do I need you for?
And the rain slaps against the window,
Oh, what can I ask of you?
And poverty whistles in the chimney,
Yeah, what do I need you for?
In the heart there's no more courage
Oh, what can I ask you?
You go to the rabbis, oh to the rabbis,
Yeah, what do I need you for?

THE QUANTUM REBBE

A re-imagination of the song *Der Filosof* ('The Philosopher') (originally *Dos Gute Kepl* by Wolf Zbarzher (1826?-1883)), satirizing claims of miracles performed by Hasidic rabbis, although some of their followers took the song as literal truth. Thus the song juxtaposes sacred and profane knowledge. Published in Eleanor Gordon Mlotek, *Mir Trogen a Gezang! Favorite Yiddish Songs of Our Generation.* Third edition, New York: Workman's Circle, 1972, p. 124. Literal translation by Norbert Hirschhorn. A traditional rendition is at http://www.youtube.com/watch?v=mNxlLVLTlBc.

Kum aher, du filosof,
Mit dayn ketsishn moykhl,
Oy, kum aher tsum rebns tish
Un lern zikh do seykhl.

A damfshif hostu oysgetrakht
Un nemst dermit zikh iber;
Der rebe shpreyt zayn tikhl oys
Un shpant dem yam ariber.

An ayznban hostu oysgeklert,
Un meynst du bist a khorets;
Der rebe shpet, der rebe lakht,
Er darf dos oyf kapores

Tsi veystu den, vos der rebe tut
Beys er zitst bekhides? –
In eyn minut in himl flit
Un pravet dort shalesh sudes.

Come here, you philosopher,*
With your cat's brain,
Oh, come to the Rebbe's table
And learn a little sense.

You invented a steamboat
And think well of yourself;
The Rebbe spreads his handkerchief
And crosses the sea.

114

You thought up the railroad,
And think you're a genius;
The Rebbe mocks, the Rebbe laughs –
He's allowed, he'll do *kapores!***

So, do you know what the Rebbe does
When he sits alone?
In one minute he flies to heaven,
And there partakes his third Sabbath meal.

*The term 'scientist' entered modern parlance only in the mid-19th century, first in English in 1833.

** Kapores is the pre-Yom Kippur custom of swinging a live chicken overhead as a symbolic sacrifice to atone for sins; here mockery.

WHEN OUR REBBE...

A re-imagination of the traditional Hasidic folksong, *Sha, Shtil* ('Shh, Be Still'), from M. Kipnis *Hundert Folks-Lider,* Buenos Aires: Central Association of Polish Jews in Argentina, 1949, p. 237. Reprinted by National Yiddish Book Center, Amherst MA, Steven Spielberg Digital Yiddish Library No. 13563, 1999. Literal translation by Norbert Hirschhorn. A raucous klezmer jam version is heard at http://www.youtube.com/watch?v=sWfn8cRX1P0.

Sha, shtil, makht nisht keyn geruder
Der rebe geyt shoyn tantsn vider;

Sha, shtil, makht nisht keyn gevald,
Der rebe geyt shoyn tantsn bald.

Un az der rebe tantst,
Tantsn mit di vent,
Lomir ale plesken mit di hent.

Sha, shtil...

Un az der rebbe tantst,
Tantst dokh mit der tish,
Lomir ale tupen mit di fis.

Sha, shtil...

Un az der rebe zingt
Dem heylikn nign
Blaybt der sotn a toyter lign.

Shh, quiet, make no disturbance,
The Rebbe is about to dance again.

Shh, quiet, raise no wild commotion,
The Rebbe is about to dance.

And as the Rebbe dances,
The walls dance with him,
Let's all clap our hands.

Shh, quiet...

And as the Rebbe dances,
Even dancing with the table,
Let's all tap our feet.

Shh, quiet...

And as the Rebbe sings
The holy melody,
The Devil will stay dead.

TRISTESSE

A re-imagination of *Di Goldene Pave* ('The Golden Peacock');
original poem by Anna Margolin (1887-1952), set to a folksong with
music and literal translation by Chava Alberstein: The Klezmatics
& Chava Alberstein, Track 14 from 'The Well'/ *Di Krenitse.* http://
www.youtube.com/watch?v=baLEGFOQDR0.

Iz di goldene pave gefloygn, gefloygn,
Un di nakht hot geefnt di goldene oygn.
Likhtiker mayner, shlof ayn.

Di nakht hot geefnt di goldene oygn,
Bin ikh a fidl gevorn un du der boygn,
Umruiker mayner, shlof ayn.

Bin ikh a fidl gevorn un du der boygn,
Un dos glik iber undz hot farlibt zikh geboygn,
Tsertlekher mayner, shlof ayn.

117

Un dos glik iber undz hot farlibt zikh geboygn,
Gelozt undz aleyn un farfloygn, farfloygn.
Troyeriker mayner, shlof ayn.

The golden peacock has flown, flown off,
And night's opened its eyes of gold.
Bright one of mine, go to sleep.

Night opened its eyes of gold,
I was the fiddle and you were the bow,
Restless one of mine, go to sleep.

I was the fiddle and you were the bow,
Fortune, enamoured, bowed down over us,
Soft one of mine, go to sleep

Fortune, enamoured, bowed down over us,
Left us alone and flew off, flew off.
Sad one of mine, go to sleep.

TO LIFE!

A re-imagination of *A Glezele Lekhayim* ('A Little Glass to
Life'), words by B. Bergholtz (n.d.); original music by Joseph
Rumshinsky (1881-1956); from Eleanor and Joseph Mlotek, *Songs
of Generations. New Pearls of Yiddish Song,* New York: Workmen's
Circle, 2004, pp. 238-9; literal translation by Norbert Hirschhorn. A
toasting song, the well-mannered original may be heard at

A glezele lekhayim, es shodt nit nemen haynt,
Ven me zitst bay a yontevdikn tish;
A glezele lekhayim far frayndshaft un far fraynd,
Me zol shtendik nor munter zayn un frish!

A glezele lekhayim far alt un yung vos zitsn do,
Un far yedern bazunder,
vos zaynen haynt mit undz nito!
A glezele lekhayim – der bekher ful mit vayn –
Far der zun, zi zol shtendik mit undz zayn!

A glezele lekhayim trinken mir atsind,
Nor oyf simkhes bay yedern fun aykh!
A glezele lekhayim, far muter un far kind,
Az mit nakhes di mame zol zayn raykh!

A glezele lekhayim nit opshteyn zol fun aykh di shayn,
Keyn shvartser tog in lebn
In der mishpokhe zol nit zayn!
A glezele lekhayim iz oystrinken keday,
Ven me zet zikh mit fraynd oyf dos nay!

A glezele lekhayim, far undzer groysn land,
Iber undz zol der himl heln reyn!
A glezele lekhayim, ich vintsh aykh nor, zol zayn,
Mit a shmeykhl oyf di lipn zolt ir geyn!

119

A glezele lekhayim, begleytn zol shtendik greyt!
Mit layblekhe un nonte me
Zol keyn mol nit zayn tsesheydt!
A glezele lekhayim – far alts, vos undz bahelt!
Un far sholem oyf der gantser velt!

A little glass to life, it doesn't do any harm to drink today
When one sits at a holiday table.
A little glass to life for friendship and friends,
May they always be lively and fresh!

A little glass to life for old and young ones sitting here,
And especially for all
Who aren't here with us today!
A little glass to life, the beaker's full of wine,
For the sun it should always be with us!

A little glass to life we'll now drink
Only at celebrations, for each one of you!
A little glass for mothers and for children,
That the mothers should be rich with pride!

A little glass to life, you shouldn't lose the glow,
May there be no dark day in the life of your families!
A little glass to life, is worthwhile to drink up,
When one sits anew with friends!

A little glass to life for our beautiful country,
The sky should be bright and pure above us!

A little glass to life, I wish you all
To go with a smile on your lips!

A little glass to life may always accompany us!
May we never be separated
From our near and dear ones!
A little glass to life for everything that brightens our lives!
And for peace over the whole world!

CONFESSIONS

A re-imagination of the song *Moyde Ani* ('I confess'). Lyrics by
Mark Schweid (1891-1969), music by Michel Gelbart (1889-1962).
http://zemerl.com/cgi-bin/print.pl?title=Moyde+Ani. The song
plays tragically on the Hebrew prayer *Modeh Ani* ('I am Thankful').
Literal translation by Norbert Hirschhorn. A beautiful rendition is
at http://www.youtube.com/watch?v=eWixVn3MGRA at 12:24, by
Abudysetty.

Moyde ani, moyde ani,
Moyde ani lefonekho
Got, mit tsorn,
Az vos fun dayn kind
Iz in der fremd gevornt!
Shvere yorn, lender file
Ikh gedenken nit mer di tfile.
Kum antkegn
Ikh bin avek dikh zukhn
Oyf fardreyte vegn.

Ikh bin nokh yung, unerfarn
S'kenen fremder mentshn mikh farnarn.

I confess, I confess,
I confess before you
God [who is] angry
That what was your child
Has become wary in an alien land!
Hard years, many lands,
I no longer remember the prayers.
Come, return,
I've been off searching for you
In perverse ways.
I'm still young, naïve,
Strangers can deceive me.

A TAILOR'S SONG

A re-imagination of the traditional humorous folk song *Hob ikh mir
a mantl* ('I Have a Coat'). Coming in several versions, this trans-
literation and literal translation from Eleanor and Joseph Mlotek.
Songs of Generations. New Pearls of Yiddish Song, New York:
Workmen's Circle, 2004, p. 106. A charming rendition by Yiddish
Theatre veteran, Leah Koenig Stolper, is at http://www.youtube.
com/watch?v=Oha_nKyi768. She speaks in Polish to a Warsaw
audience.

Hob ikh mir a mantl fun fartsaytikn tukh,
Tra-la-la-la, la-la-la-la, la, la, la

Iz in im nishto keyn gantsener dukh,
Tra-la-la-la,...
Darum hob ikh zikh batrakht
Un fun dem mantl a rekl gemakht.
Tra-la-la-la-, la, la, la,
Un fun dem mantl a rekl gemakht.

Hob ikh mir a rekl fun fartsaytikn tukh...
Iz in im nishto keyn gantsener dukh...
Darum hob ikh zikh batrakht
Un fun dem rekl a vestl gemakht...

hitl, keshene, henger, shnipsel, lidl...

I have a coat made of ancient cloth,
Tra-la-la-la, la-la-la-la, la, la, la
Without a whole piece of material.
Tra-la-la-la,...
So I reflected on what to do –
And made the coat into a jacket.
Tra-la-la-la-, la, la, la,
And made the coat into a jacket.

I have a jacket made of ancient cloth,
Without a whole piece of material.
So I reflected on what to do –
And made the jacket into a vest....

hat, pocket, loop, bowtie, a little song...

123

AUTHOR'S NOTE: Yiddish does not use capital letters, but for consistency I've capitalized all first words in a line in both the transliterations and the translations, as is done in the collections by the Mloteks.

ACKNOWLEDGEMENTS

'Basherte' in *Magma* (UK)
'Cave Song', 'To Life!', 'From My Mouth' (as 'Raisins with
Almonds') in *PN Review* (UK)
'Ten Brothers' in *South Bank Poetry* (UK)
'Make a Living' in *Brittle Star* (UK)
'Three Sisters' in *Café Review* (US)
'Jump Rope Songs', 'My Cousin the Greenhorn' in *Modern
Poetry in Translation* (UK)
'From Podwoloczyska to Ellis Island','Mayn Rue-Platz' in
Acumen (UK)
'The Last Branch Dreams of Release', 'Tristesse' in
Monastery of the Moon (Dar al-Jadeed, Beirut, 2012)
'The Wandering Jew', 'Sleep My Child', 'A Czarist Conscript
Bids Farewell' in *Agenda* (UK)

I am grateful to Lee Gould, Jacqueline Saphra – fine poets,
dear friends – for their review of the poems and manuscript
in drafts; to my mentors – Dannie Abse, Frank Bidart, Roger
Weingarten; to my publisher Bernadette Jansen op de Haar for
her belief in the work; and to Cynthia, for everything.

Particular appreciation goes to Khayke Beruriah Wiegand,
Woolf Corob Lector in Yiddish, Oxford Centre for Hebrew
and Jewish Studies (University of Oxford), for her meticulous
corrections of source materials. Any remaining errors are
entirely mine.

PUBLISHER'S ACKNOWLEDGEMENTS

The publisher has attemped, within reason, to contact all copyright holders and thanks them for their permission to reprint the relevant transliterations and literal translations of song texts.

Detailed acknowledgements for each song text are printed in the *Sources, transliterations, literal translations, links to music section.*

About The Author

Norbert Hirschhorn is a physician specializing in international public health, commended in 1993 by President Bill Clinton as an 'American Health Hero'. He now lives in London and Beirut. His poems have been published in over three dozen journals and three full collections: *A Cracked River*, Slow Dancer Press, London, 1999; *Mourning in the Presence of a Corpse*, Dar al-Jadeed, Beirut, 2008; *Monastery of the Moon*, Dar al-Jadeed, Beirut, 2012. His work has won a number of prizes in the US and UK. See his website: www.bertzpoet.com.

Holland Park Press is a unique publishing initiative. It gives contemporary Dutch writers the opportunity to be published in Dutch and English. We also publish new works written in English and translations of classic Dutch novels.

To

- Find out more
- Learn more about Norbert Hirschhorn
- Discover other interesting books
- Read our unique Anglo-Dutch magazine
- Practice your writing skills
- Take part in discussions
- Or just make a comment

Visit www.hollandparkpress.co.uk